WORLD IN PERIL

OCEANS
UNDER THREAT

PAUL MASON

Heinemann Library
Chicago, Illinois

www.heinemannraintree.com
Visit our website to find out
more information about
Heinemann-Raintree books.

To order:

☎ Phone 888-454-2279
💻 Visit www.heinemannraintree.com
to browse our catalog and order online.

Edited by Louise Galpine and Rachel Howells
Designed by Richard Parker and Manhattan Design
Picture research by Hannah Taylor and Rebecca Sodergren
Production by Alison Parsons

Printed in China by Leo Paper Products Ltd.

13 12 11 10 09
10 9 8 7 6 5 4 3 2 1

Library of Congress Cataloging-in-Publication Data
Mason, Paul.
  Oceans under threat / Paul Mason.
    p. cm. -- (World in peril)
  Includes bibliographical references and index.
  ISBN 978-1-4329-2286-3 (hc) -- ISBN 978-1-4329-2293-1
(pb)
  1. Marine pollution--Juvenile literature. I. Title.
  GC1090.M37 2008
  333.91'64--dc22
                          2008037082

Acknowledgments

We would like to thank the following for permission to
reproduce photographs: Coastal Concern Action Group pp. **24**
and **25** (Mike Page); Corbis pp. **19** (Brooks Kraft), **23** (Ashley
Cooper); Eyevine p. **26** (Jiri Rezac); FLPA p. **10** (Reinhard
Dirscherl); Getty Images pp. **4** (Paul Chelsey), **14** (Guang Niu),
15 (Clive Mason), **17** (Igor Garin/Epsilon); Mary Evans Picture
Library p. **6**; naturepl p. **11** (Georgette Douwma); Paul Mason
p. **7**; Photolibrary pp. **8** (Animals Animals/ Shane Moore),
12 (image100), **16** (Corbis), **18** (Nicholas Pitt), **20** (Radius
Images), **21** (JW.Alker), **22** (David Kirkland); REUTERS p. **27**
(Jayanta Shaw JS/AH); Still Pictures pp. **9** (Lineair), **13** (David
Tapia Munoz/ UNEP).

Cover photograph of phytoplankton bloom made up of
diatoms, the base of the marine food chain, Sea of Cortez,
Mexico, reproduced with permission of FLPA (Minden
Pictures/ Norbert Wu).

We would like to thank Michael Mastrandrea for his invaluable
help in the preparation of this book.

Every effort has been made to contact copyright holders of
material reproduced in this book. Any omissions will be
rectified in subsequent printings if notice is given to
the publishers.

All the Internet addresses (URLs) given in this book were valid
at the time of going to press. However, due to the dynamic
nature of the Internet, some addresses may have changed, or
sites may have changed or ceased to exist since publication.
While the author and publishers regret any inconvenience this
may cause readers, no responsibility for any such changes can
be accepted by either the author or the publishers.

Contents

How Do the Oceans Keep Us Alive? 5

Why Was Yesterday's Catch So Much Bigger
    Than Today's? 6

How Is the Ocean Being Stripped of Fish? 8

How Does Fishing Threaten This Seabed? 10

How Clean Are the Oceans? 12

How Did Algae Nearly Stop the Olympics? 14

How Can Pollution Ruin This Seashore? 16

Is It Safe to Go in the Sea? 18

What Makes This Coral So Fragile? 20

Could the Sea Swallow Up These Islands? 22

What Ate Away This Coast? 24

How Can We Help the Oceans? 26

Review Questions 28

Glossary *30*

Find Out More *31*

Index *32*

Some words are printed in bold, **like this**. You can find out what they mean by looking in the glossary.

How Do the Oceans Keep Us Alive?

Without oceans, we would all be dead. The oceans provide us with food. Ocean-going ships carry goods and people between **continents**. Of course, we also enjoy swimming, surfing, and sailing in oceans. Most important of all, the oceans feed **moisture** to rain clouds. They help keep the planet at the right temperature for life to survive.

Oceans cover more than 70 percent of our planet. In the past, the oceans have seemed limitless. Whatever people did, the oceans stayed the same. The seas had clean water and were full of fish.

Today, though, there are more people on Earth than ever before. Our **pollution**, our giant fishing fleets, and the changes humans have caused to Earth's **climate** are putting the oceans under threat.

This giant catch of salmon was made on the Fraser River in Canada. In the past, there were lots of fish in the seas and rivers. River **fisheries** like this one, and sea fisheries such as the Grand Banks in the North Atlantic, produced huge quantities of fish. There was plenty of money to be made as a fisherman, and some people became wealthy as a result.

During the 1900s, the world's population grew, and more people began to eat fish. Each year, bigger boats with bigger nets took increasingly large catches from the sea. In the end, the fish began to run out. The catches got smaller and smaller, and some fisheries – for example, the Grand Banks – had to close. No one is sure if the size of catches will ever increase again.

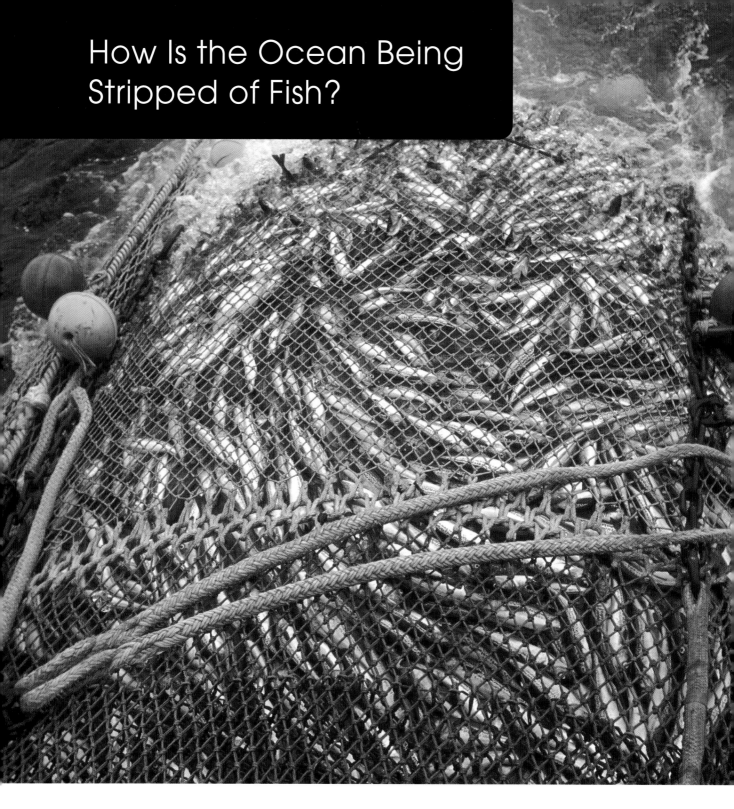

How Is the Ocean Being Stripped of Fish?

How many fish do you think are caught up in this net? Nets like this one can catch tons of fish every day. This includes unwanted types of fish that are thrown back and young fish that have not had the chance to **reproduce**.

If one fish lays its eggs and is then caught, the number of fish stays the same. But when a fish is caught before it has had a chance to lay its eggs, it means there will be fewer fish in the sea.

What effect are these fishermen in Sri Lanka having on the number of fish in the sea? They are each using a hook and line to catch fish, so fewer fish are caught. Also, if the fishermen catch smaller, younger fish by accident, they can throw them back.

There are other ways to fish apart from hook-and-line fishing. For example, using smaller nets means catches are smaller. Nets with larger holes allow young fish to escape.

How Does Fishing Threaten This Seabed?

How would you like to go snorkeling above this seabed? The seabed around our shores is home to an amazing variety of living creatures. Wherever light reaches the sea bottom, fish, seaweed, corals, and other creatures live. All these creatures depend on one another. Small fish take shelter among the weeds or corals, darting out to eat **plankton**. Bigger fish **prey** on the smaller fish. Shellfish feed on **nutrients** floating in the water.

This fishing net has become wrapped around a reef, which is dying. Lost nets are not the only threat to life on the ocean floor. **Bottom-trawling** boats drag their nets across the seafloor, scooping up fish. The nets scrape the seabed. They rip up the seaweeds, smash down reefs, and rip shellfish from their homes. In deep water, where there are fewer living things, and creatures grow more slowly, the seabed may never recover.

How Clean Are the Oceans?

Like this tropical beach, the sea is naturally clean. Almost all sea life needs clean water in order to stay fit and healthy.

People have been using the sea as a garbage can for hundreds of years. They pump **sewage** and other waste into it every day. Until recently, this did little harm. The oceans are huge, and most of the waste broke down and disappeared without doing any long-term damage.

This is sewage being pumped into the sea. Can you imagine going for a swim here? Each year, the world's growing population pumps more and more waste into the sea. Poisonous chemicals, sewage, and other **pollution** mix in the world's oceans. There, they kill off plants and animals. This upsets the delicate balance of ocean life. Millions of tons of plastic garbage have also now collected in our oceans.

How Did Algae Nearly Stop the Olympics?

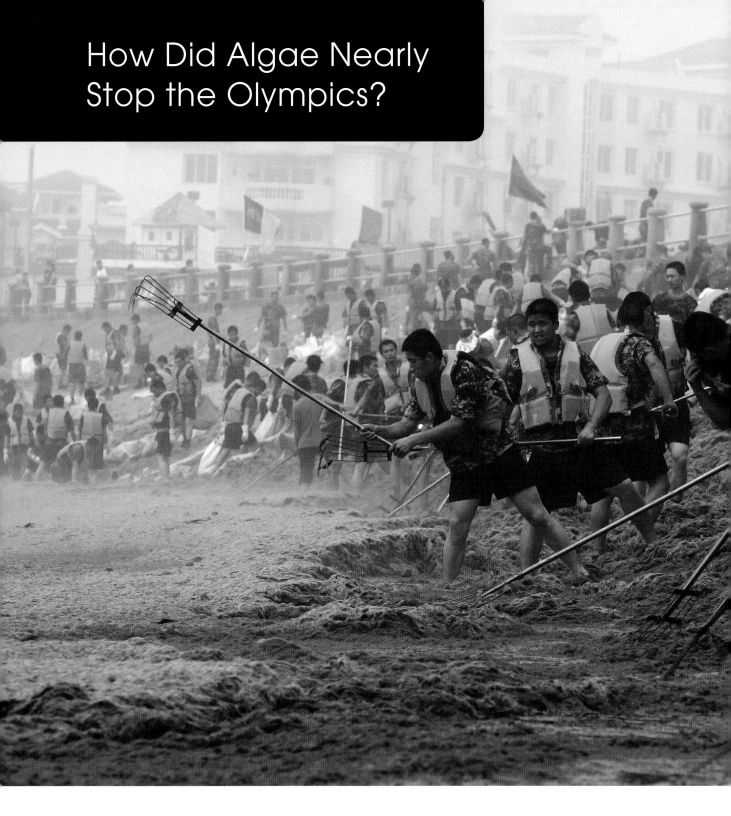

Can you imagine sweeping up green, slimy **algae** like this? In June 2008, a nasty shock awaited sailors practicing for the Beijing Olympic Games. The sea was clogged by tons of algae! Thousands of people had to help clear it.

This is known as an algal bloom. The bloom is a disaster for animals. The fast-growing algae use up all the oxygen in the water. Without enough oxygen, fish and other plants die.

In the end, the algae was cleared away in time for the Olympic sailing races. But what had caused the algae to appear?

Algal blooms have been happening for many years. Today, they seem to be happening more often than in the past. At the same time, increasing amounts of **fertilizer** have been washed from farmland into the oceans by rainfall. Many people think that fertilizer is one cause of algal blooms.

This otter is resting in a bed of **kelp**—or, he was until the photographer disturbed him! Like other ocean animals and plants, otters rely on clean seas for food. They spend much of their time in the water looking for food.

Can you imagine a type of **pollution** that, in just a few hours, can destroy food in the ocean?

This bird is coated with oil. The oil spilled into the ocean from an oil tanker off the coast of Ukraine in 2007. With heavy, oil-coated feathers, the bird cannot fly or keep itself warm. If it tries to clean itself, it will end up swallowing oil, which will poison it.

The fish that birds and other animals rely on for food were also poisoned by the oil. Tens of thousands of animals and plants were killed.

Is It Safe to Go in the Sea?

Would you rather be reading this book on a warm, sunny beach? Most people would! Since the early 1900s, many people have enjoyed a day at the beach as a way of relaxing.

Swimming in the sea first became popular because the salty seawater was thought to be refreshing and healthy. Today, millions of people each year visit the beach on a day trip or on a vacation.

This beach is at Crystal River, Florida. There is nothing crystal about it, though—the beach has been closed because of **pollution**.

Beaches are often closed in this way. During heavy storms, **sewers** overflow their **sewage** straight into the sea. Accidents and spills from factories release chemicals into the rivers and seas. Papermaking plants release chemicals that dye the waves pink.

What Makes This Coral So Fragile?

How many colors can you spot on this coral reef? Coral reefs are very popular with divers. The bright colors of the coral look beautiful. They are also home to some amazing sea creatures.

In some places, the anchors of dive boats have damaged the reefs. Divers sometimes break off pieces of coral as souvenirs, even though this is banned. But these are not the only threats facing coral reefs today.

This coral reef is suffering from **bleaching**. Bleaching is caused by a rise in the water temperature. Coral gets its color from **algae**. Algae are tiny plants that live in the coral. The algae also provide the coral with food. If the water temperature rises, the corals push out the algae. Unless the water temperature cools again, the corals die. Many experts have linked coral bleaching to **global warming**, which is increasing ocean temperatures.

Could the Sea Swallow Up These Islands?

Tropical islands like Vanuatu, in the South Pacific Ocean, are many people's dream vacation destination. They have warm weather, regular rainfall, and beautiful plants. On some islands there are **rare** animals, which cannot be seen anywhere else on Earth. Madagascar, for example, is an island off the coast of Africa. It was once home to the amazing elephant bird. The elephant bird weighed twice as much as an ostrich. No wonder it could not fly!

Pollution is causing a rise in the world's **average** temperature. This is known as **global warming**. As temperatures rise, water that was once frozen melts and flows into the sea. This causes sea levels around the world to slowly rise.

It is thought that Tuvalu could be one of the first countries to disappear because of **climate** change. Twelve thousand people could be driven from their homes.

What Ate Away This Coast?

How would you like to live right on the ocean's edge? The owners of these homes must have been delighted when they moved in. Living near the sea gave them fresh air, beautiful views, and a beach on their doorsteps.

But living by the sea can also mean being **exposed** to violent storms. Many scientists think that these storms are happening more often because of **global warming**.

This photograph was taken just four years after the one on the left. In a short space of time, several buildings and half the backyards have been eaten away by the sea.

Land is worn away when powerful storms whip up waves that wear away the bottom of the cliff. The top then collapses into the sea and is washed away. In some places, 2 meters (6.5 feet) of land are washed away each year.

How Can We Help the Oceans?

Can you imagine being in a tiny boat like this one, at risk of falling into the freezing ocean if the giant ship hits you? These supporters of an organization called Greenpeace were trying to stop Japanese whaling ships in the Southern Ocean in 2008. These ships hunt and kill whales to sell for money. Greenpeace had helped to bring an end to whaling in 1985. But not all countries agreed to stop. Greenpeace also works to stop **bottom-trawling**.

These fishermen in India say their catches have dropped in recent years. If they sell less fish they make less money, and may go hungry.

Is it possible to help the oceans and fishermen by going shopping? Some fish come from **sustainable fisheries**. Iceland's cod fishery, for example, is run sustainably. This means that the fishermen never take too many fish. Buying Icelandic cod means you are helping the ocean's stocks of cod to survive.

WHAT DID YOU FIND OUT ABOUT THE OCEANS?

How are the oceans keeping us all alive?
Hint: The oceans are full of water, and without water humans cannot survive. Of course, we cannot drink seawater—so why are oceans important to our water supplies?

What happens when everyone eats the same type of fish?
Hint: The photographs on pages 6 and 7 might be a good place to start trying to answer this question. Pages 8 and 11 might also be helpful.

What role do the oceans play in the world's climate?
Hint: **Climate** is the typical weather for a certain location. Think about the things in the oceans that are affected by the weather and temperature.

How might the oceans be affected if the world's climate changes?
Hint: Try to think of what would happen if ocean temperatures rose or fell. Pages 21, 23, and 25 might all be useful in trying to find an answer.

Will there still be coral reefs for our grandchildren to dive on? Why is this?
Hint: Pages 20 and 21 should give you some ideas. List some reasons for whatever you decide.

How does farming affect the oceans?
Hint: Even though farming takes place on land, it can affect the oceans, from Australia's Great Barrier Reef to the Florida Keys, and all sorts of places in between. The photograph of the Chinese coast on page 14 will help you find out how.

Why do people use the oceans as garbage dumps?
Hint: You can see the effect of dumping trash into the oceans on page 13. But if we did not put it there, where would we put it? Lots of people refuse to have garbage dumps near their homes—are they right to do so?

Would you like to live beside the seaside? Why?
Hint: Living near a beach sounds like a great idea, especially if you enjoy swimming and water sports. But look again at the photographs on pages 13, 17, 19, 23, and 25—are you sure? To help you decide, make two lists, one discussing the good things and one discussing the bad things about living by the sea.

What are some things you can do to help the oceans stay healthy?
Hint: These might not all be obvious. For example, if changes to the climate harm the oceans, are there things you could do to prevent the climate from changing? Could changing what you eat help the oceans?

Glossary

algae tiny plants that grow in water or moist ground

average typical amount or size. For example, if most 12-year-olds are between 4 ½ and 5 ½ feet tall, their average height is 5 feet.

bleaching removing the color from something

bottom-trawling way of fishing in which nets are dragged along the seabed

climate typical or average weather conditions for a place. For example, rain forests have a wet climate, and deserts have a dry climate.

continent large landmass. There are seven continents: Europe, North America, South America, Africa, Asia, Australia, and Antarctica.

exposed unprotected or without shelter

fertilizer chemical added to soil to help plants grow. Chemicals washed off the soil and into rivers and oceans can affect the plants and animals that live there.

fishery area of the sea in which fish are often caught

global warming rise in Earth's average temperature. Most scientists agree that global warming has mainly been caused by human activity.

kelp large, brown seaweed

moisture wetness

nutrient combination of chemicals that is needed for living things to grow or repair themselves. Plants get some of their nutrients from the soil they grow in.

plankton small living creatures that live on or near the surface of the sea. They provide food for other animals, ranging from tiny fish to giant basking sharks and whales.

pollution dirt that harms the environment

prey animal or animals that are hunted by others as food

rare unusual; not found very often

reproduce make offspring or young. When dogs have puppies, they are reproducing.

sewage human toilet waste mixed with water

sewer tunnel that carries sewage away to be disposed of safely

sustainable produced in a way that does not harm the environment

Find Out More

Books

Chambers, Catherine, and Nicholas Lapthorn. *Mapping Earthforms: Oceans and Seas*. Chicago: Heinemann Library, 2008.

Day, Trevor. *Life in the Crusher: Mysteries of the Deep Oceans*. Mankato, Minn.: Capstone, 2009.

Gray, Susan H. *Biomes: Oceans*. Mankato, Minn.: Compass Point, 2001.

Lynch, Emma. *Food Webs: Ocean Food Chains*. Chicago: Heinemann Library, 2005.

DVD

The Blue Planet (2001), narrated by David Attenborough, took over a year to make and is still the best documentary series about the oceans and their creatures.

Websites

www.fishonline.org/search/simple

Find out which fish you can eat without harming the oceans.

www.greenpeace.org/usa/campaigns/oceans

This section of the **environmental** group Greenpeace's website is about oceans. You can follow links to explore topics such as whales and the future of fishing. This web page also includes a useful section listing recent news developments about oceans.

www.panda.org/news_facts/education/middle_school/habitats/oceans

WWF's web page about oceans contains basic information, plus links to other related subjects.

Index

algae 14–15, 21
algal bloom 14, 15
animals 16–17, 22

beaches 12, 18–19, 24
birds 17, 22
bottom-trawling 11, 26

chemical spills 13, 19
climate change 5, 21, 23, 24
coastline, disappearing 24–25
cod 27
corals 10, 20–21
  bleaching 21

farmland 15
fertilizers 15
fish 5, 10, 14, 17
fish eggs 8
fishing industry 5, 6–9, 11, 26–27
  hook-and-line fishing 9
  sustainable fisheries 27
  whaling 26
floods 23

global warming 21, 23, 24
Grand Banks 6–7
Greenpeace 26

hook-and-line fishing 9

islands 22

kelp 16

living by the sea 24–25

Madagascar 22

nets 8, 9, 11
nutrients 10

oil spills 17
otters 16
oxygen 14

papermaking plants 19
plankton 10
plastic garbage 13
pollution 5, 16–17, 19, 23
  chemical spills 13, 19
  oil spills 17
  plastic garbage 13
  sewage 12, 13, 19

rainfall 15
reefs 11, 20–21
reproduction 8

sailing 15
seabed 10, 11
sea levels 23
seaweeds 10, 11
sewage 12, 13, 19
sewers 19
shellfish 10, 11
ships 5
  bottom-trawling boats 11, 26
  whaling ships 26
snorkeling 10, 20
Sri Lanka 9
storms 24, 25

vacations 18, 22
Vanuatu 22

waste 12, 13
water temperature 21
whaling 26